Survey of Credit Underwriting Practices

2008

Office of the Comptroller of the Currency

June 2008

Contents

Survey of Credit Underwriting Practices
2008

Introduction

The Office of the Comptroller of the Currency (OCC) conducted its 14th annual underwriting survey to identify trends in lending standards and credit risk for the most common types of commercial and retail credit offered by national banks. The survey covered the 12-month period ending March 31, 2008.

The 2008 survey included examiner assessments of credit underwriting standards at the 62 largest national banks.[1] This population covers loans totaling $3.7 trillion as of December 2007, approximately 83 percent of total loans in the national banking system. Large banks referenced in the subsequent comments are the 20 largest banks by asset size supervised by the OCC's Large Bank Supervision department; the other 42 banks are supervised by the OCC's Midsize/Community Bank Supervision department.

OCC examiners assigned to each bank assessed overall credit trends for 20 commercial and retail credit products. For purposes of this survey, commercial credit includes the following 13 categories:
- agricultural,
- asset-based lending,
- commercial construction,
- residential construction,
- other commercial real estate,
- commercial leasing,
- international,
- large corporate,
- leveraged,
- middle market,
- small business,
- hedge funds – direct lending exposure, and
- hedge funds – counterparty credit exposure.

Retail credit includes the following seven categories:
- affordable housing,
- credit cards,
- indirect consumer paper,
- conventional home equity,
- high loan-to-value (HLTV) home equity,
- other direct consumer, and
- residential first mortgages.

---

[1] The OCC increased the asset threshold for banks in this year's survey from $2 billion to $3 billion.

The term "underwriting standards," as used in this report, refers to the terms and conditions under which banks extend or renew credit, such as financial and collateral requirements, repayment programs, maturities, pricing, and covenants. Conclusions about "easing" or "tightening" represent OCC examiners' observations during the survey period. A conclusion that the underwriting standards for a particular loan category have eased or tightened does not necessarily indicate that all the standards for that particular category have been adjusted. Rather, it suggests that the adjustments that did occur had the net effect of easing or tightening the aggregate conditions under which banks extended credit.

Part I of this report summarizes the overall results of the survey. Part II depicts the survey results in graphs and tables.

Part I: Overall Results

Primary Findings

- After four consecutive years of eased underwriting standards, the majority of the banks surveyed tightened underwriting standards for both commercial and retail loans.
- Primary reasons for tightened standards included the overall economic outlook, the downturn in residential real estate, a changing risk appetite, and a decrease in market liquidity.
- Examiners reported that risk in both the commercial and retail portfolios has increased over the past 12 months, and they expect portfolio risk to continue to increase over the coming year.
- Key factors that contributed to the rise in product and portfolio credit risk were the weakening economy, rising energy costs, turbulence in the secondary credit markets, the downturn in the housing market, and the anticipated impact of relaxed underwriting standards over the past few years on payment performance.

Commentary on Credit Risk

After several years of increasingly accommodative credit terms, the financial market disruption in 2007 caused an abrupt change in risk appetite and a renewed focus on fundamental credit principles by bank lenders.

Banks and other investors have suffered major losses resulting from the disruption in their ability to distribute both commercial and retail credit exposures during the past year. The subsequent tightening of credit underwriting standards – higher credit spreads, more financial covenants, less borrower leverage – is the expected response to the mark-to-market losses on the held for sale portfolio as well as investors' more thorough assessment of credit risk. Notwithstanding the recent overall tightening of standards, examiners anticipate that the relaxed underwriting standards of the past, coupled with current economic weaknesses, will result in increased credit risk and losses over the next 12 months.

The OCC expects that the lessons learned from the recent market turbulence will lead to more prudent underwriting standards for both commercial and retail credit exposures. The OCC emphasizes that it is important for bankers to maintain and enforce prudent credit underwriting standards throughout the economic cycle, both when financial market liquidity is robust and when it is poor. While the competitive environment will inevitably cause changes in credit underwriting standards, banks need to have risk management and control processes to signal when standards veer away from safe and sound banking practices. Banks should underwrite credit based upon an expectation that the borrower can repay the loan, regardless of whether the loan is intended for portfolio or for distribution. As recent events have clearly shown, liquidity conditions in credit markets can change abruptly. Banks originating credit for distribution should maintain underwriting standards reasonably consistent with the standards for their own portfolio holdings.

Commercial Underwriting Standards

After four years of eased underwriting standards, examiners reported net tightening of commercial credit standards for the 12 months ending March 31, 2008. The 2008 survey results indicate that more than half of the surveyed banks tightened commercial underwriting standards, more than triple the number of banks reported to have tightened in 2007. Only 6 percent of the surveyed banks eased commercial standards, down significantly from 2007. The table below summarizes the changes.

Commercial Products				
	2005	2006	2007	2008
Eased	34%	31%	26%	6%
Unchanged	54%	63%	58%	42%
Tightened	12%	6%	16%	52%

Examiners overwhelmingly cited growing concerns about the economy as the leading reason for more stringent standards. While the economic outlook was a main concern for all commercial products, it was particularly pronounced for commercial real estate (CRE) products. For larger institutions, the disruption in financial markets during the second half of 2007 had a significant impact on the leveraged finance and syndicated loan markets. Examiners cited market liquidity most frequently as the reason banks tightened standards for large corporate and leveraged loans, as well as international and hedge fund exposures.

Credit spreads, or the compensation for assuming credit risk, have risen sharply. Banks have emphasized maintenance financial covenants and lower borrower leverage, as well as increased guarantor support requirements.

Selected Product Trends

Underwriting standards tightened for all commercial loan products surveyed, with over 60 percent of the banks strengthening in at least one product line. The most prevalent tightening occurred in CRE loans, leveraged loans, and counterparty credit exposure to hedge funds. Examiners reported a few isolated instances of eased commercial credit underwriting standards.

Commercial Real Estate

CRE products include commercial construction, residential construction, and other CRE loans. These products are offered by virtually all of the surveyed banks. Net tightening, which measures the difference between the percentage of banks tightening and those easing, was greatest in residential construction, followed by commercial construction. The following tables provide the breakdown by each real estate type.

Commercial Residential Construction				
	2005	**2006**	**2007**	**2008**
Eased	21%	25%	17%	2%
Unchanged	72%	64%	50%	36%
Tightened	7%	11%	33%	62%

Commercial Construction				
	2005	**2006**	**2007**	**2008**
Eased	29%	32%	29%	8%
Unchanged	63%	56%	59%	43%
Tightened	8%	12%	13%	49%

Other Commercial Real Estate				
	2005	**2006**	**2007**	**2008**
Eased	24%	32%	20%	2%
Unchanged	65%	60%	73%	73%
Tightened	11%	8%	7%	25%

Examiners most often cited the following as reasons for strengthening of CRE underwriting standards:
- A weakening economy, specifically the downturn in residential real estate markets.
- Declines in market values/prices as a result of oversupply or slow-moving inventory.
- Existing credit concentrations, both by type of product and by location.
- Use of non-traditional terms and excessive investor speculation.

CRE remains a primary concern among examiners given the rapid growth of these exposures and banks' significant concentrations relative to their capital. These concerns are compounded by elevated concerns over market conditions in select areas.

Leveraged Loans

Underwriting standards for leveraged loans at the 15 banks in the survey that offered such loans changed significantly in 2007. The easing examiners had noted in the 2006 and 2007 surveys continued until the sharp disruption in financial markets that began last summer. Since that time, most banks have responded to investor concerns and the negative economic outlook by tightening underwriting terms, particularly those relating to pricing, covenants and maximum allowable leverage. However, because banks committed to a number of transactions prior to the market turbulence, there are instances where banks continue to negotiate transactions where underwriting standards are weak. Given that the volume of new transactions has declined significantly since last summer, it is not clear whether the changes in underwriting standards are a temporary reaction to troubled market conditions or a longer term return to more prudent fundamental credit risk principles.

Leveraged Loans				
	2005	**2006**	**2007**	**2008**
Eased	32%	62%	67%	20%
Unchanged	68%	30%	33%	20%
Tightened	0%	8%	0%	60%

Counterparty Credit Risk

A third product for which banks have tightened credit terms is counterparty credit exposure to hedge funds. While few banks have such exposures (seven banks out of 62), those that do are systemically important institutions and the terms of credit for these counterparties can influence overall liquidity in financial markets. Banks strengthened underwriting standards by raising initial margin requirements and imposing stronger collateral requirements in response to decreased market liquidity, poor overall market conditions, a slowing economy, a decreased risk appetite, and changes in their own financial condition.

Hedge Funds Counterparty Credit Exposure		
	2007	**2008**
Eased	0%	0%
Unchanged	71%	29%
Tightened	29%	71%

Originate to Hold versus Originate to Sell

The OCC added new questions to the 2008 survey to assess any differences in underwriting between loans originated to hold in the bank's own loan portfolio and loans originated to sell in the marketplace. Of the 62 banks surveyed, 27 percent originate loans both to hold and to sell. The products that these banks originate for dual purposes represent only 19 percent of the total product responses. Examiners indicate that the majority of the loans originated in the various product lines are generally underwritten with the same standards. When standards differed, banks have typically mitigated risks of loss by enforcing conservative limits on exposures held.

The most notable difference in underwriting standards is for leveraged loans. Typically, leveraged loans underwritten with the intention to sell had weaker terms than loans originated to hold for investment. Examiners noted significant differences in loan covenants, maturities, amortization periods and fees. The tightening of underwriting standards for leveraged loans originated to sell was the direct result of changes in the economic outlook and market liquidity.

Product	Underwritten Differently	
	Yes	**No**
Leveraged Loans	67%	33%
Agricultural	50%	50%
International	40%	60%
Asset-Based Loans	33%	67%
Large Corporate	21%	79%
CRE – Other	20%	80%
CRE – Commercial Construction	20%	80%
CRE – Residential Construction	17%	83%

Retail Underwriting Standards

Examiners noted tightening of retail underwriting standards in 68 percent of the surveyed banks citing economic factors as the major basis for the change. No examiners reported overall easing of retail underwriting standards, although some easing was noted in specific products. This is a major change from the past three surveys when examiners reported overall easing at 20 percent or more of the surveyed banks and overall tightening at 13 percent or less.

Retail Products				
	2005	**2006**	**2007**	**2008**
Eased	28%	28%	20%	0%
Unchanged	62%	65%	67%	32%
Tightened	10%	7%	13%	68%

Examiners reported increased retail credit risk in at least one product at 76 percent of the surveyed banks. This increased level of risk was most pronounced in credit card and home equity lending. Examiners cited concerns about the continued downturn in residential property values and general economic conditions as the bases for increased risk levels. Examiners expect retail credit risk to continue to increase over the next 12 months at 88 percent of the banks, particularly in home equity and credit card portfolios.

Selected Product Trends

In this year's survey, examiners reported tightening of credit standards in a significant number of the surveyed retail loan products. In fact, the responses indicated tightened standards for 46 percent of retail loan products, and no change in the standards for 48 percent. Examiners noted easing of standards for only 6 percent of retail loan products.

As shown in the tables below, tighter underwriting standards were most prevalent in residential real estate and home equity lending products. No banks eased standards for residential real estate loans, and only one bank eased standards for home equity lending (both conventional and high LTV). That bank has since tightened its requirements. Examiners stated that underwriting standards for residential lending-related products tightened mainly because of the dramatic changes in economic conditions.

Residential Real Estate				
	2005	**2006**	**2007**	**2008**
Eased	22%	26%	19%	0%
Unchanged	73%	69%	67%	44%
Tightened	5%	5%	14%	56%

Home Equity – High LTV				
	2005	**2006**	**2007**	**2008**
Eased	24%	37%	22%	6%
Unchanged	56%	63%	61%	6%
Tightened	20%	0%	17%	89%

Home Equity - Conventional				
	2005	**2006**	**2007**	**2008**
Eased	27%	34%	19%	2%
Unchanged	62%	64%	66%	46%
Tightened	12%	2%	16%	52%

Where examiners noted tightening, more stringent collateral requirements were cited most frequently, closely followed by scorecard changes and documentation requirements. This conclusion was influenced by the responses on real estate-related lending products, which are the most prevalent products offered by the surveyed banks.

Easing was centered in indirect consumer lending products, for which examiners noted loosening in five of the 25 banks reporting. Relaxed standards typically involved lengthened terms and higher advance rates.

Originate to Hold versus Originate to Sell

National banks originate most retail credit products to hold. At the product level, 69 percent of products were originated exclusively to hold. Another 28 percent of the products were originated both to hold and to sell. Only 3 percent were originated exclusively to sell. Products held and sold, and sold only, were primarily residential mortgages and affordable housing loans. Surveyed banks typically originated residential mortgage and home equity loans primarily from retail branches. Broker and correspondent channels, combined, accounted for 16 percent of residential mortgage originations and 8 percent of home equity loans.

In most banks that originated both to hold and to sell, the underwriting standards for the two groups of originations did not differ. In banks whose underwriting standards for the two groups did differ, the primary differences were in pricing and fees.

Part II: Graphs and Tables

Overall Commercial Credit Underwriting Trends

Percent of Surveyed Banks

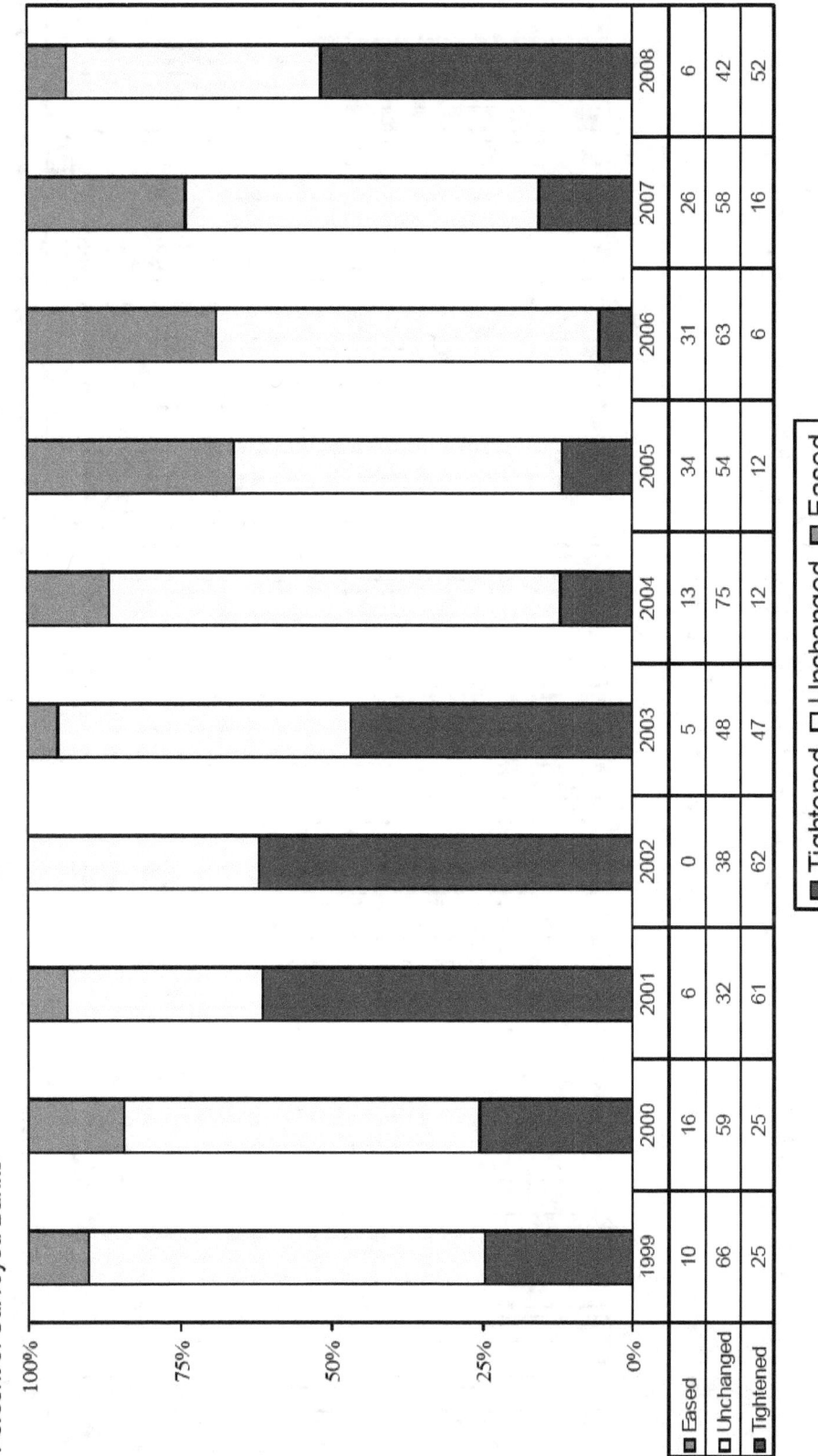

	1999	2000	2001	2002	2003	2004	2005	2006	2007	2008
Eased	10	16	6	0	5	13	34	31	26	6
Unchanged	66	59	32	38	48	75	54	63	58	42
Tightened	25	25	61	62	47	12	12	6	16	52

■ Tightened ☐ Unchanged ■ Eased

Commercial Underwriting Trends

By Product Type

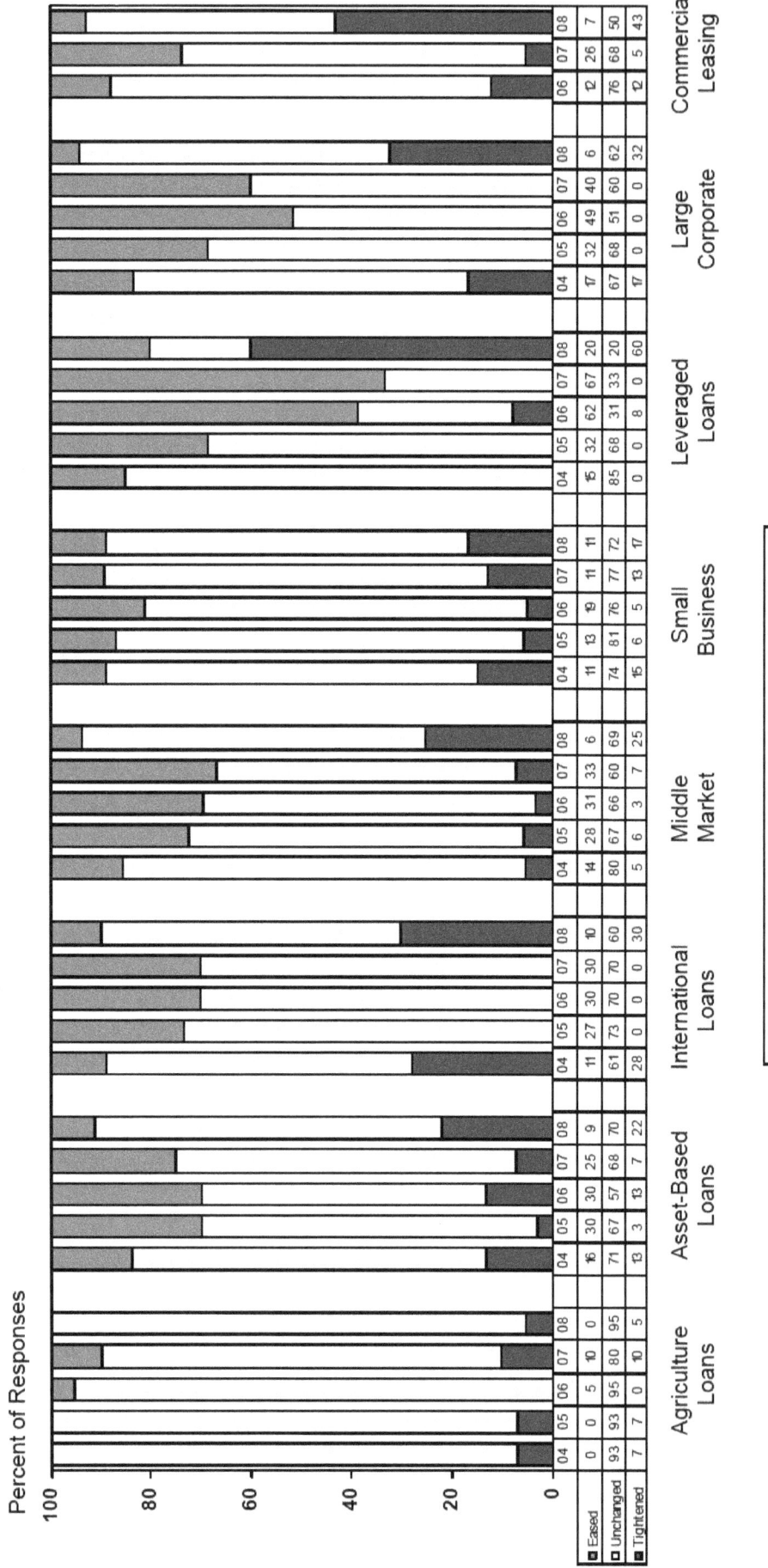

Commercial Underwriting Trends

By Product Type

Percent of Responses

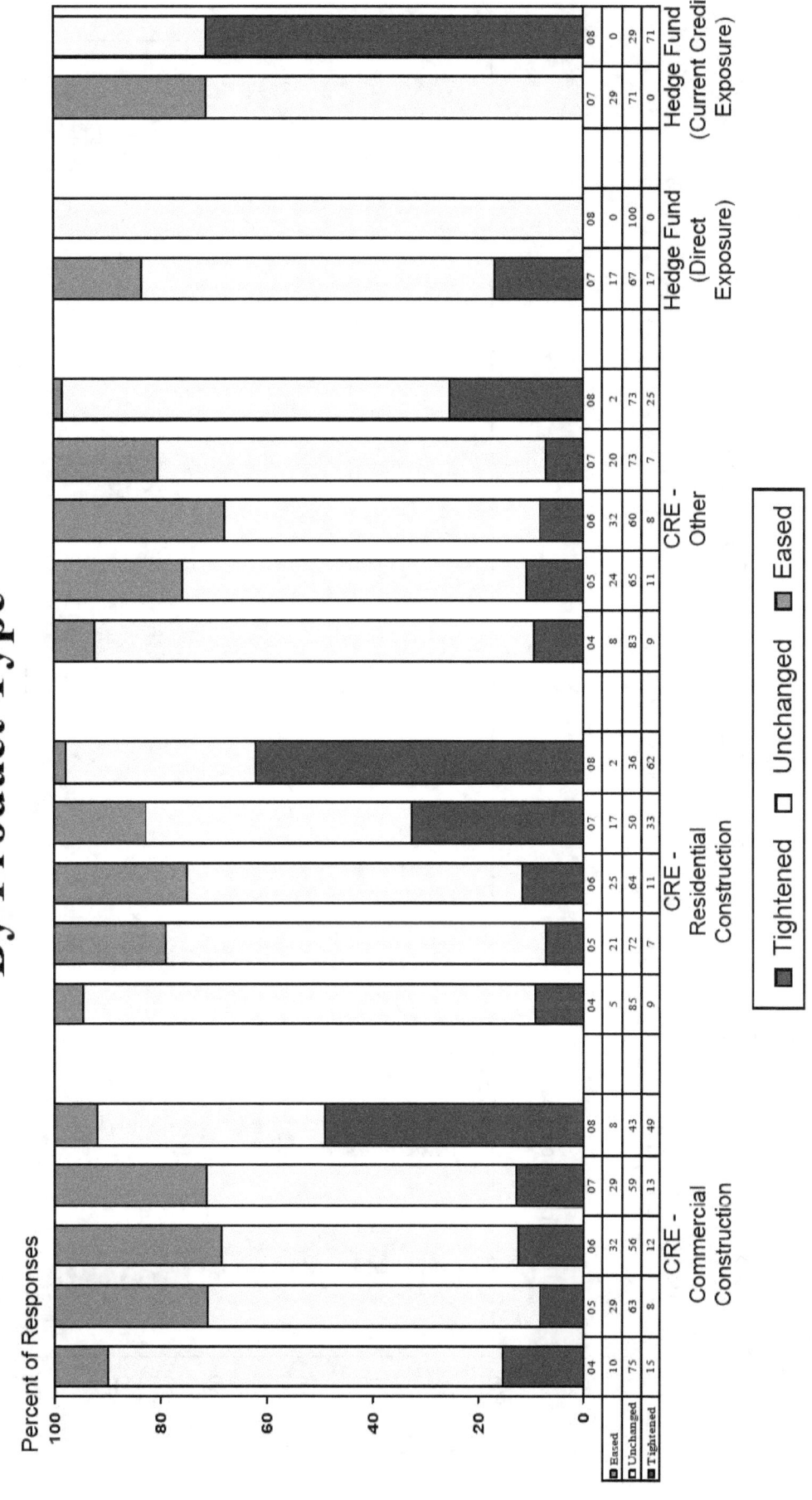

		CRE - Commercial Construction						CRE - Residential Construction					CRE - Other					Hedge Fund (Direct Exposure)		Hedge Fund (Current Credit Exposure)	
	04	05	06	07	08		04	05	06	07	08		04	05	06	07	08		07	08	07	08
Eased	10	29	32	29	8		5	21	25	17	2		8	24	32	20	2		17	0	29	0
Unchanged	75	63	56	59	43		85	72	64	50	36		83	65	60	73	73		67	100	71	29
Tightened	15	8	12	13	49		9	7	11	33	62		9	11	8	7	25		17	0	0	71

■ Tightened   □ Unchanged   ■ Eased

Survey of Credit Underwriting 2008

11

Reasons for Changing
Commercial Underwriting Standards

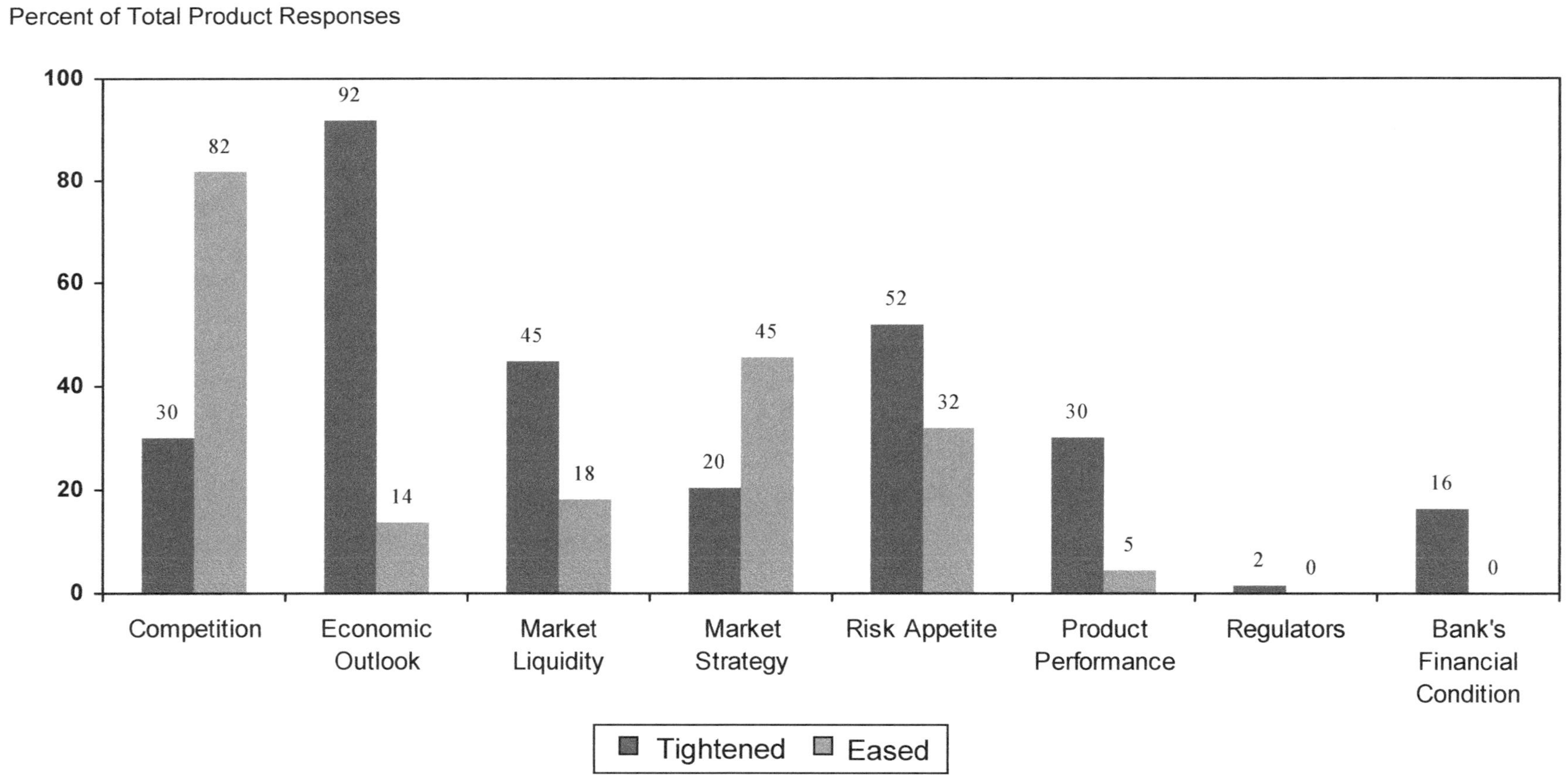

Percent of Total Product Responses

	Competition	Economic Outlook	Market Liquidity	Market Strategy	Risk Appetite	Product Performance	Regulators	Bank's Financial Condition
Tightened	30	92	45	20	52	30	2	16
Eased	82	14	18	45	32	5	0	0

■ Tightened   ■ Eased

Methods Used to Change
Commercial Underwriting Standards

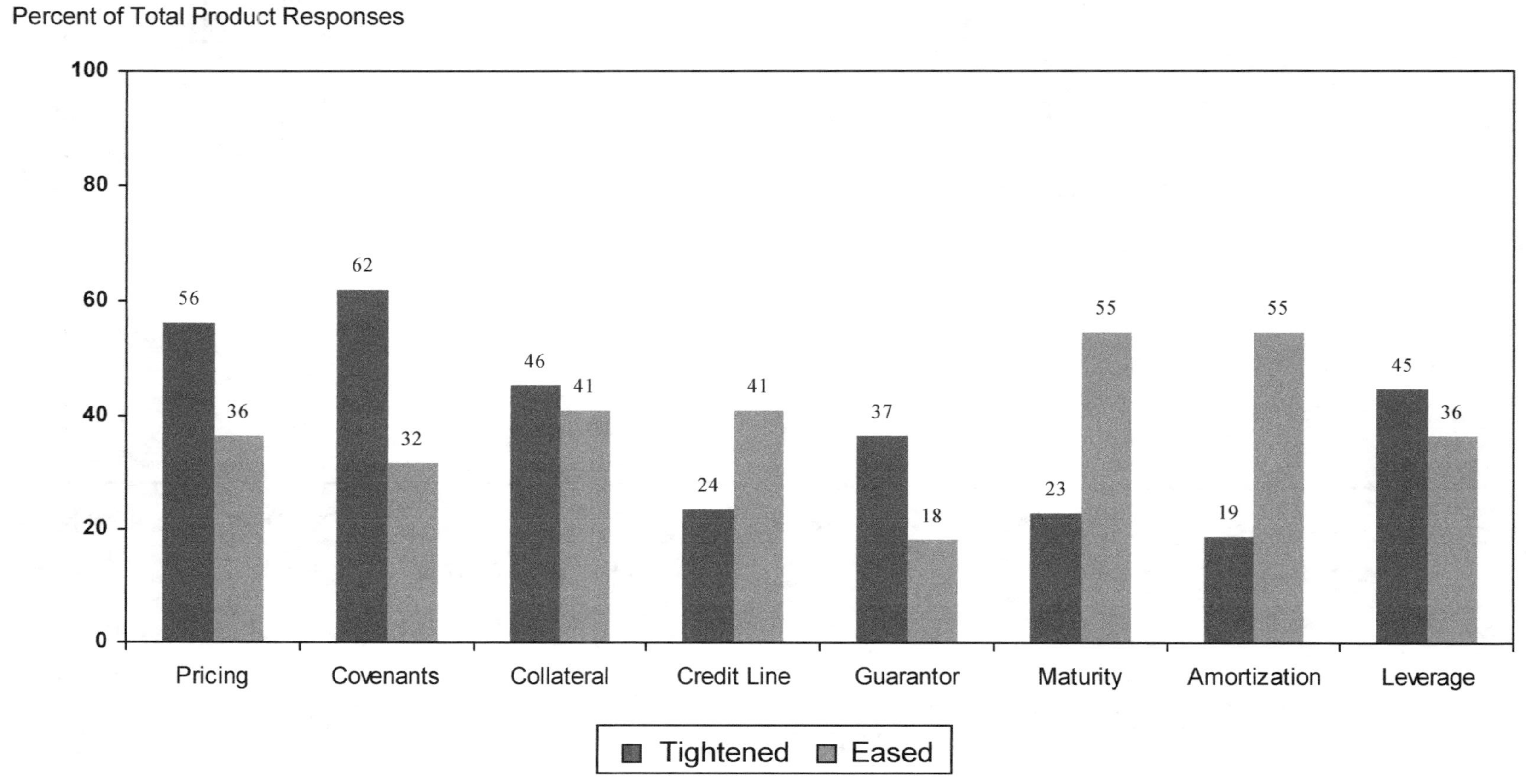

Percent of Total Product Responses

Legend: ■ Tightened ■ Eased

Method	Tightened	Eased
Pricing	56	36
Covenants	62	32
Collateral	46	41
Credit Line	24	41
Guarantor	37	18
Maturity	23	55
Amortization	19	55
Leverage	45	36

Survey of Credit Underwriting 2008

Commercial Credit Risk Trends

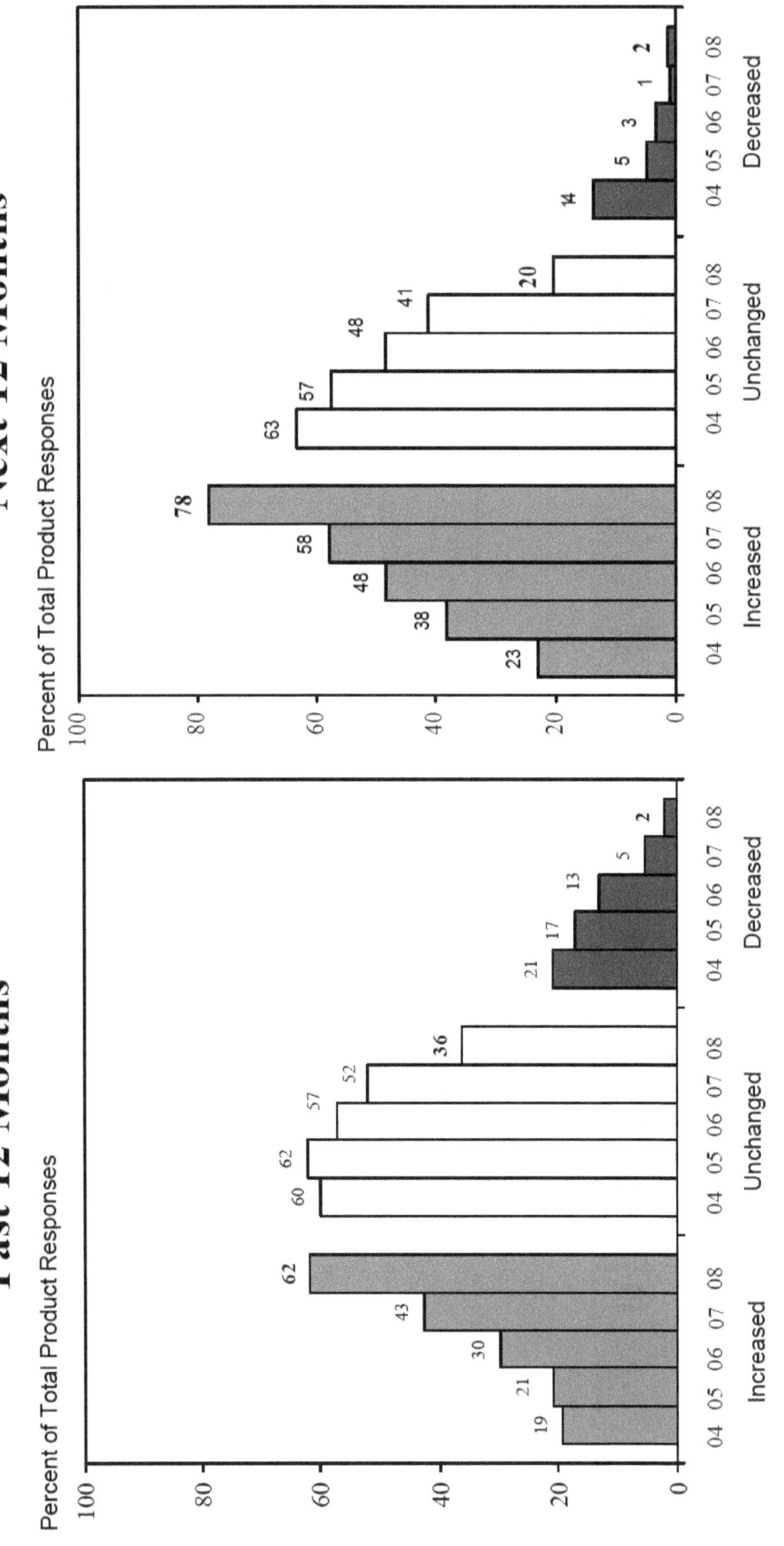

Past 12 Months

Percent of Total Product Responses

Next 12 Months

Percent of Total Product Responses

Survey of Credit Underwriting 2008

14

Commercial Credit Risk Trends

Current Credit Risk Change by Product Type

Percent of Responses

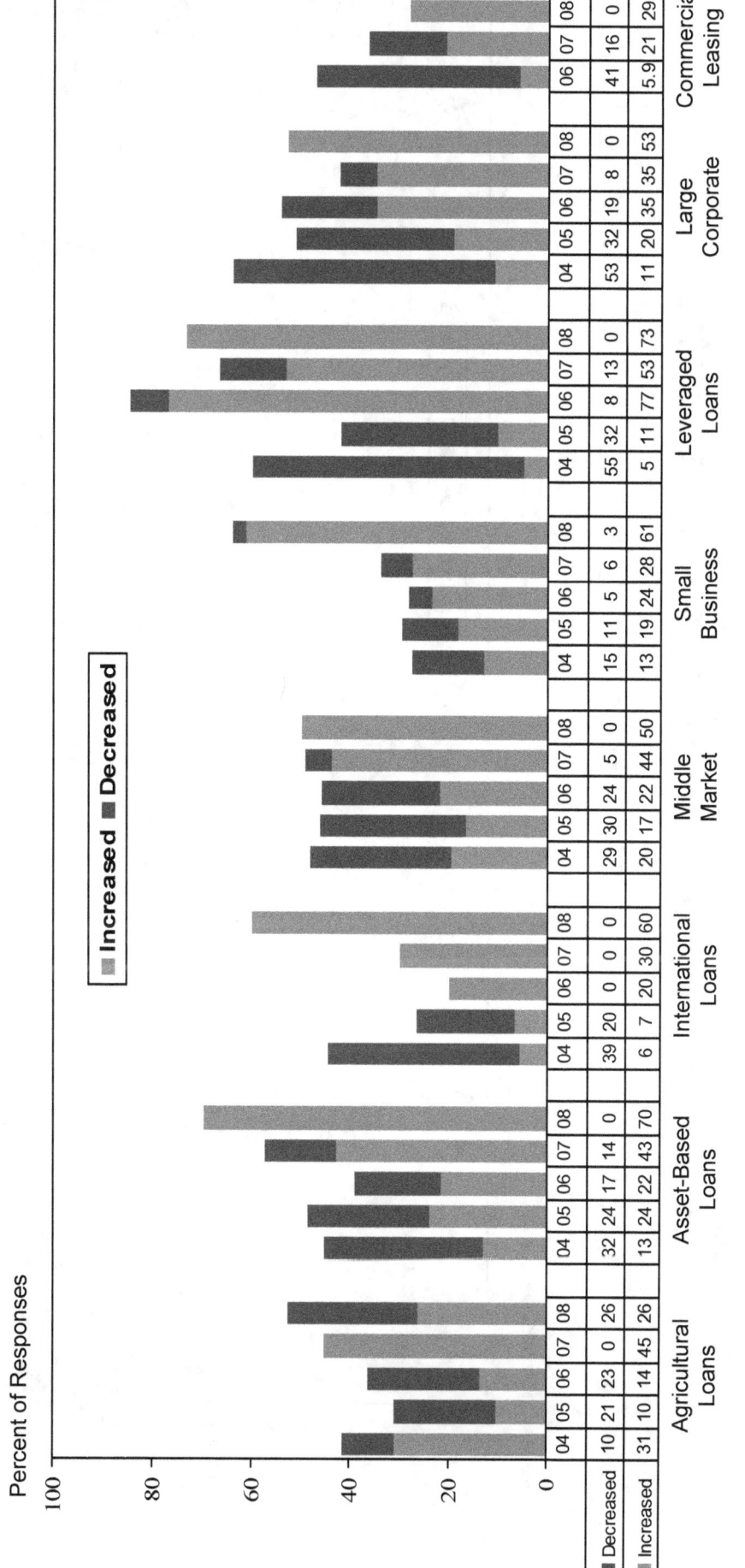

	Increased	Decreased

	04	05	06	07	08		04	05	06	07	08		04	05	06	07	08		04	05	06	07	08		04	05	06	07	08		04	05	06	07	08		06	07	08
Decreased	10	21	23	0	26		32	24	17	14	0		39	20	0	0	0		29	30	24	5	0		15	11	5	6	3		55	32	8	13	0	53	32	19	8	0	41	16	0
Increased	31	10	14	45	26		13	24	22	43	70		6	7	20	30	60		20	17	22	44	50		13	19	24	28	61		5	11	77	53	73	11	20	35	35	53	5.9	21	29
	Agricultural Loans						Asset-Based Loans						International Loans						Middle Market						Small Business						Leveraged Loans					Large Corporate					Commercial Leasing		

Survey of Credit Underwriting 2008

15

Commercial Credit Risk Trends

Current Credit Risk Change by Product Type

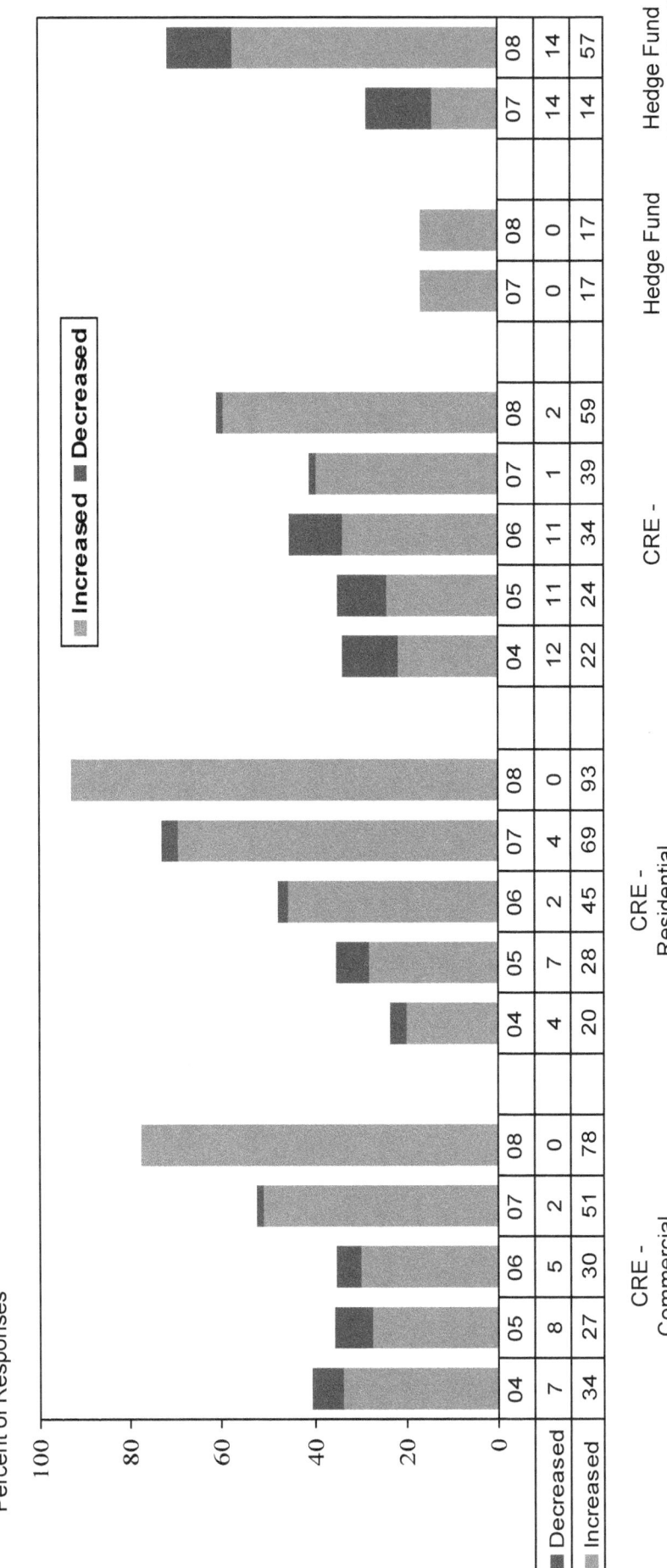

Percent of Responses

Legend: ■ Increased ■ Decreased

	Decreased	Increased
04	7	34
05	8	27
06	5	30
07	2	51
08	0	78

CRE - Commercial Constructions

	Decreased	Increased
04	4	20
05	7	28
06	2	45
07	4	69
08	0	93

CRE - Residential Constructions

	Decreased	Increased
04	12	22
05	11	24
06	11	34
07	1	39
08	2	59

CRE - Other

	Decreased	Increased
07	0	17
08	0	17

Hedge Fund (Direct Exposure)

	Decreased	Increased
07	14	14
08	14	57

Hedge Fund (Current Credit Exposure)

Overall Retail Credit Underwriting Trends

Percent of Surveyed Banks

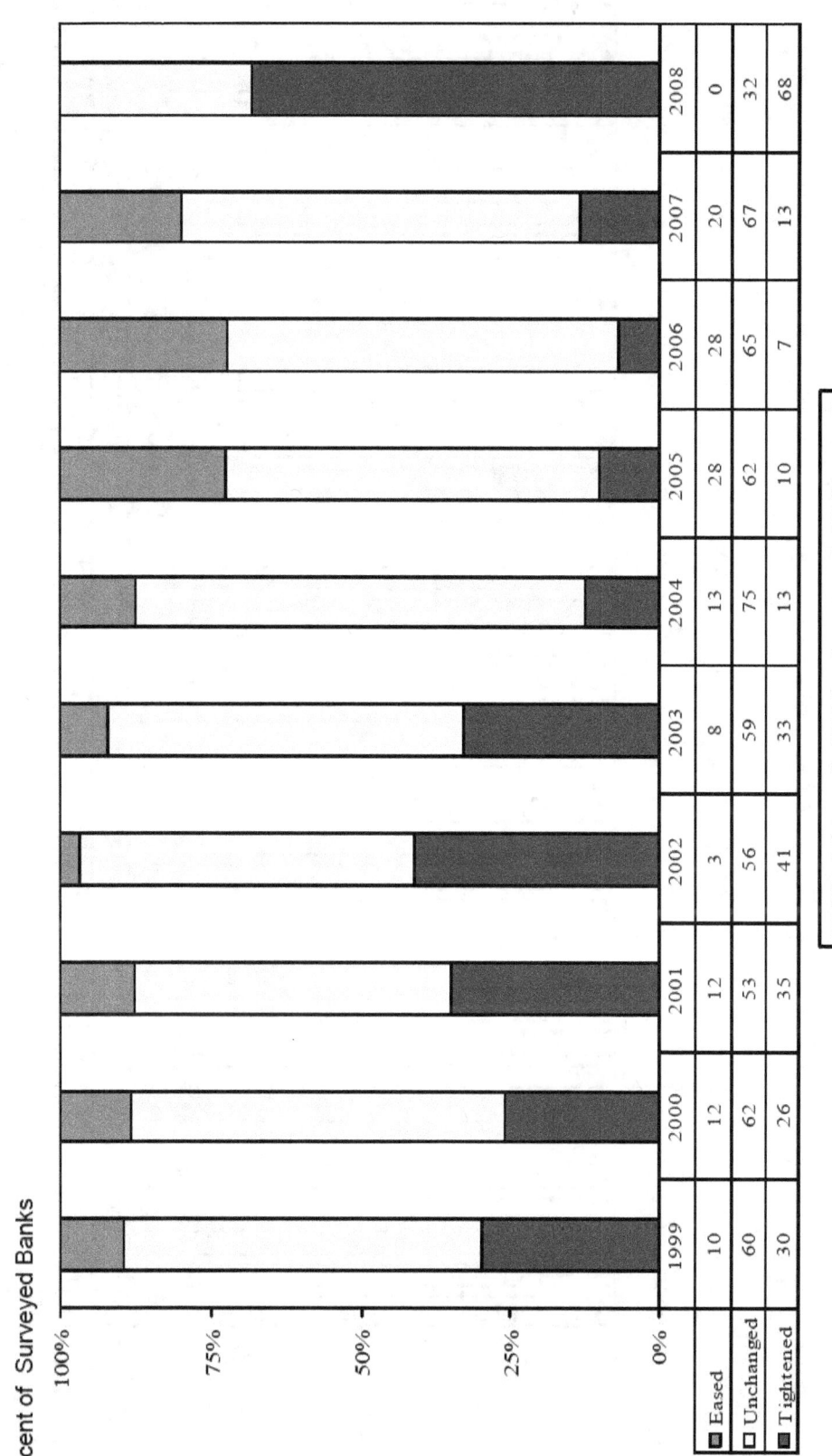

	1999	2000	2001	2002	2003	2004	2005	2006	2007	2008
Eased	10	12	12	3	8	13	28	28	20	0
Unchanged	60	62	53	56	59	75	62	65	67	32
Tightened	30	26	35	41	33	13	10	7	13	68

■ Tightened □ Unchanged ■ Eased

Survey of Credit Underwriting 2008

17

Retail Underwriting Trends

By Product Type

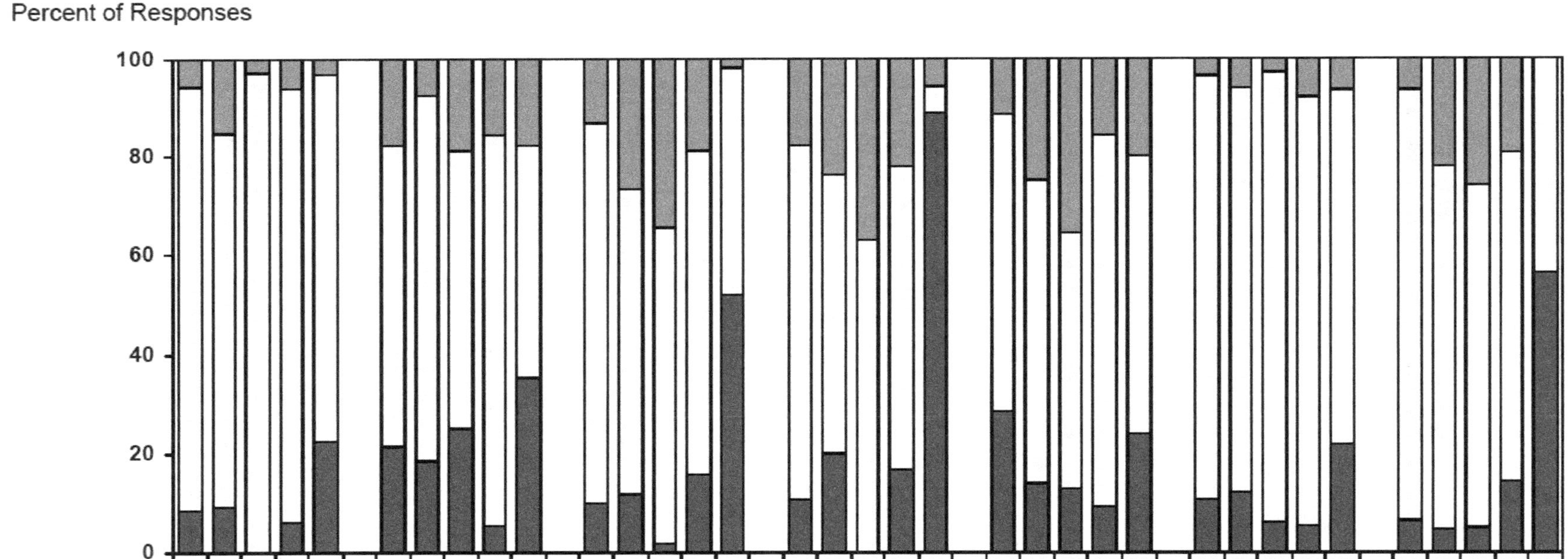
Percent of Responses
100
80
60
40
20
0

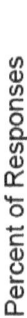

Affordable Housing

	04	05	06	07	08
Eased	6	15	3	6	3
Unchanged	86	76	97	88	74
Tightened	9	9	0	6	23

Credit Cards

	04	05	06	07	08
Eased	18	7	19	16	18
Unchanged	61	74	56	79	47
Tightened	21	19	25	5	35

Home Equity Conventional

	04	05	06	07	08
Eased	13	27	34	19	2
Unchanged	77	62	64	66	46
Tightened	10	12	2	16	52

Home Equity High LTV

	04	05	06	07	08
Eased	18	24	37	22	6
Unchanged	71	56	63	61	6
Tightened	11	20	0	17	89

Indirect Consumer

	04	05	06	07	08
Eased	11	25	35	16	20
Unchanged	60	61	52	75	56
Tightened	29	14	13	9	24

Other Direct Consumer

	04	05	06	07	08
Eased	4	6	3	8	6
Unchanged	86	82	91	87	72
Tightened	11	12	6	5	22

Residential Real Estate

	04	05	06	07	08
Eased	6	22	26	19	0
Unchanged	87	73	69	67	44
Tightened	6	5	5	14	56

■ Tightened □ Unchanged ■ Eased

Reasons for Changing
Retail Underwriting Standards

Percent of Total Product Responses

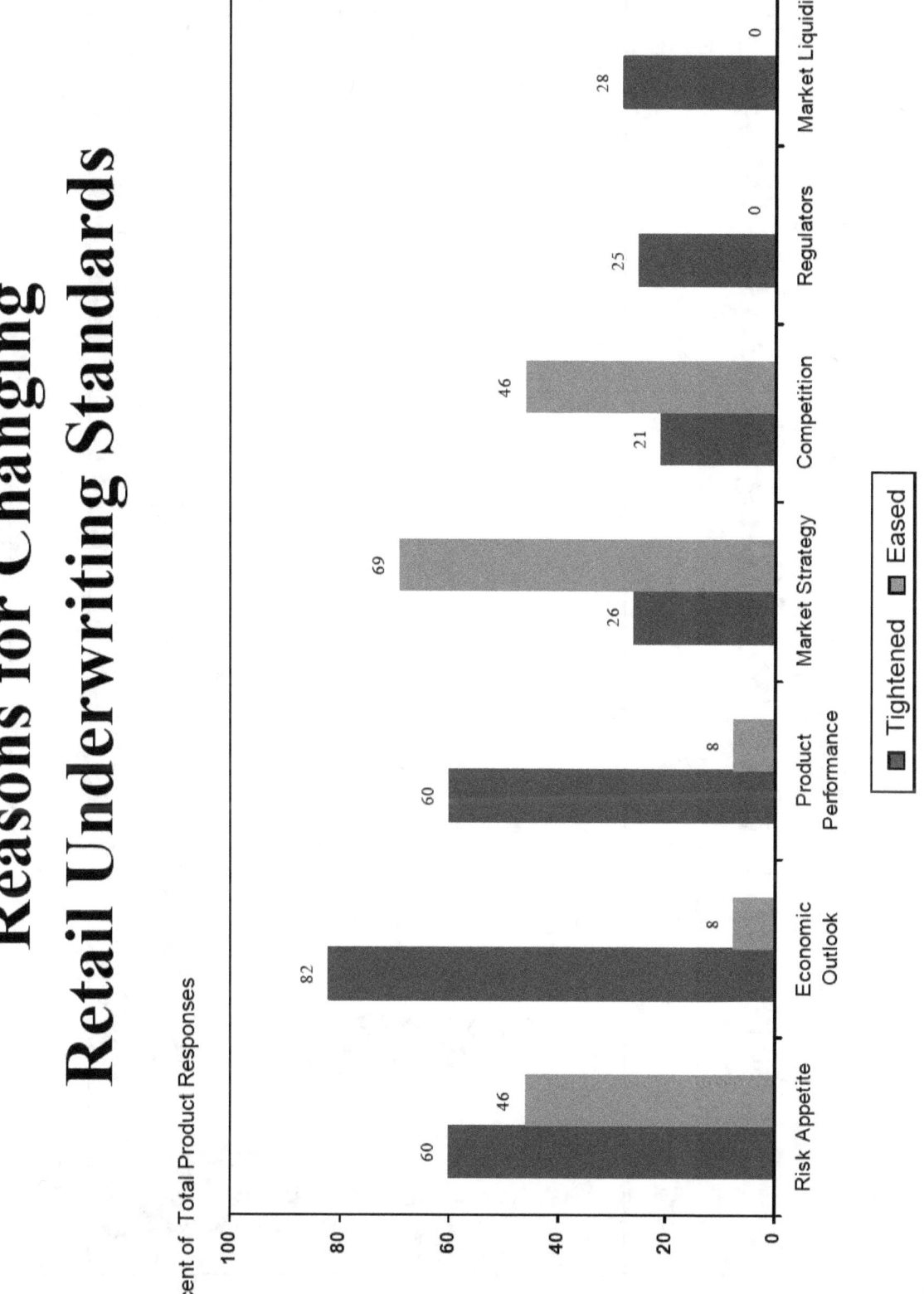

Survey of Credit Underwriting 2008

Methods Used to Change Retail Underwriting Standards

Percent of Total Product Responses

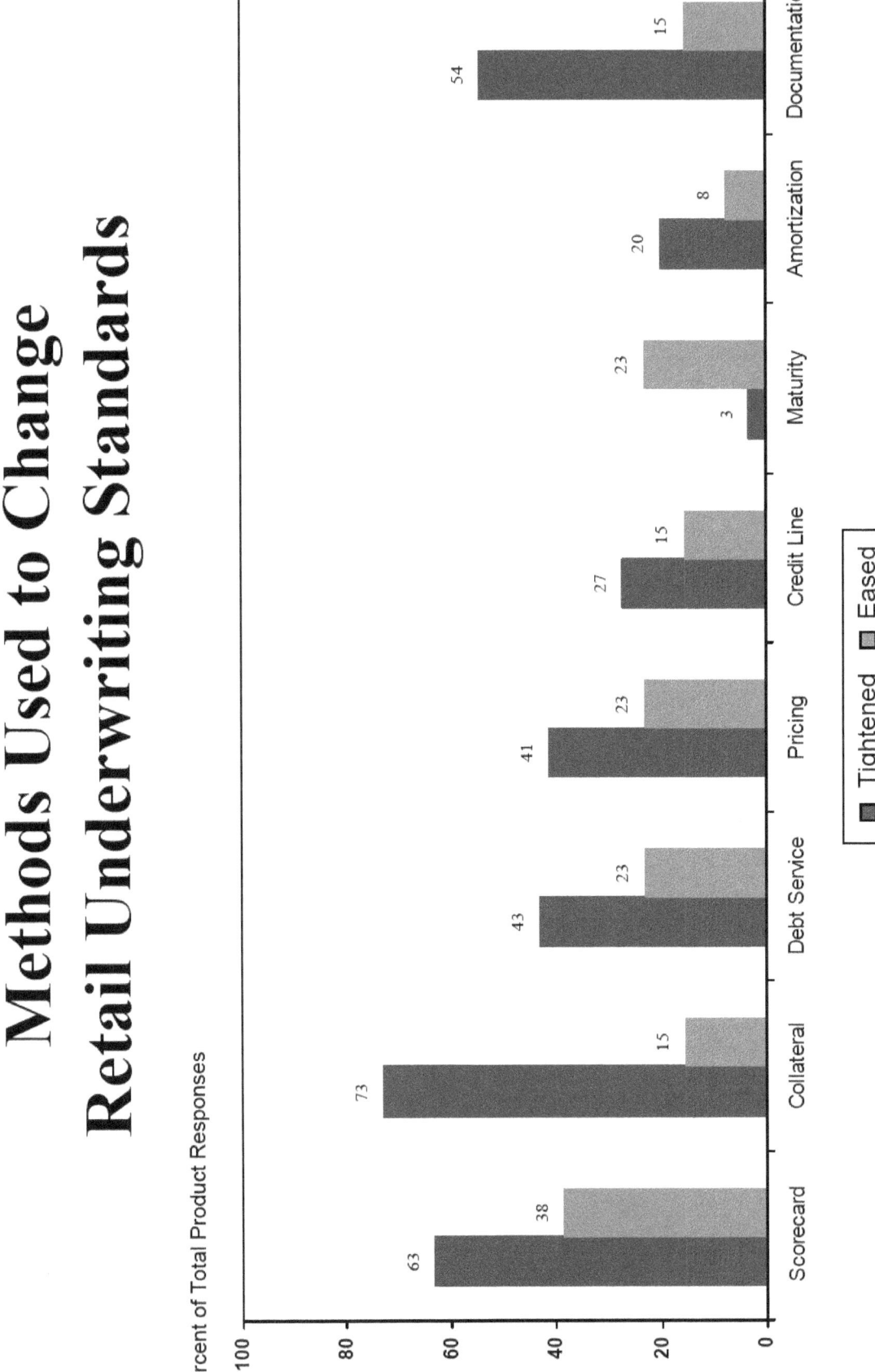

Legend: ■ Tightened ■ Eased

Scorecard: Tightened 63, Eased 38
Collateral: Tightened 73, Eased 15
Debt Service: Tightened 43, Eased 23
Pricing: Tightened 41, Eased 23
Credit Line: Tightened 27, Eased 15
Maturity: Tightened 3, Eased 23
Amortization: Tightened 20, Eased 8
Documentation: Tightened 54, Eased 15

Retail Credit Risk Trends

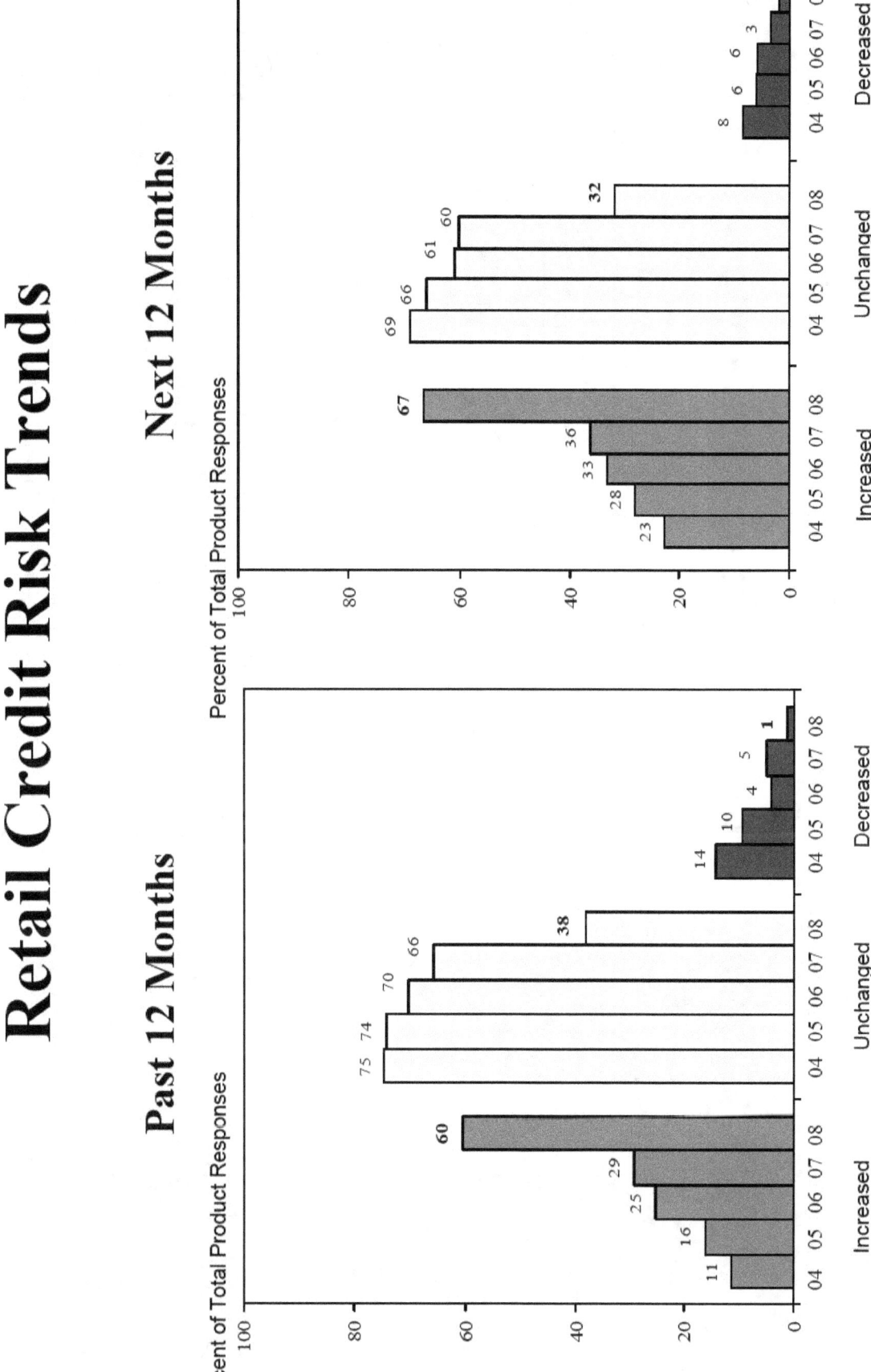

Past 12 Months

Percent of Total Product Responses

Next 12 Months

Percent of Total Product Responses

Survey of Credit Underwriting 2008

21

Retail Credit Risk Trends

Current Credit Risk Change by Product Type

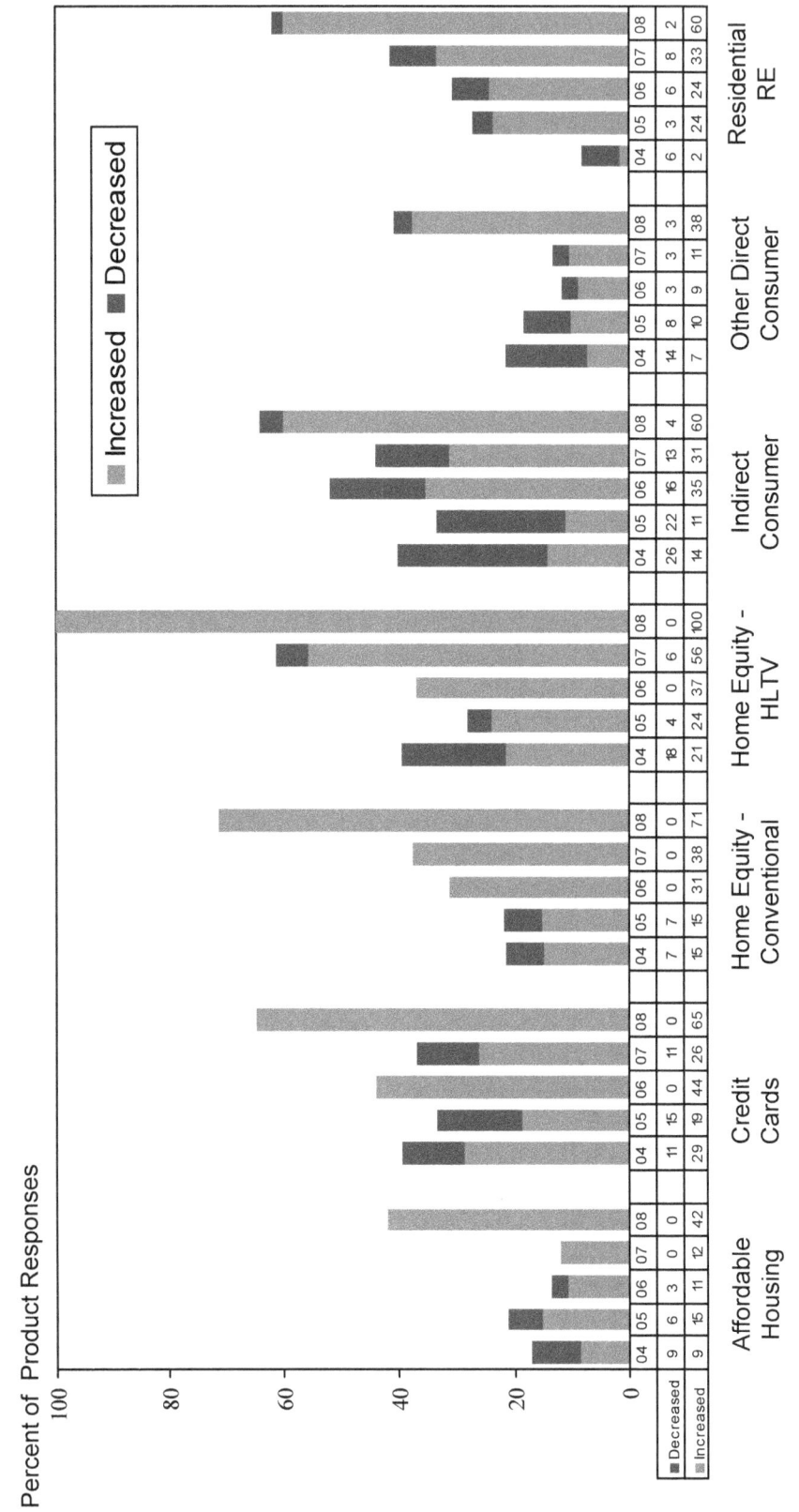

Percent of Product Responses

Legend: ■ Increased ■ Decreased

	04	05	06	07	08		04	05	06	07	08		04	05	06	07	08		04	05	06	07	08		04	05	06	07	08		04	05	06	07	08		04	05	06	07	08
Decreased	9	6	3	0	0		11	15	0	11	0		7	7	0	0	0		18	4	0	6	0		26	22	16	13	4		7	8	3	3	3		6	3	6	8	2
Increased	9	15	11	12	42		29	19	44	26	65		15	15	31	38	71		21	24	37	56	100		14	11	35	31	60		7	10	9	11	38		2	24	24	33	60

Affordable Housing | Credit Cards | Home Equity - Conventional | Home Equity - HLTV | Indirect Consumer | Other Direct Consumer | Residential RE

Survey of Credit Underwriting 2008

22

Origination Purpose

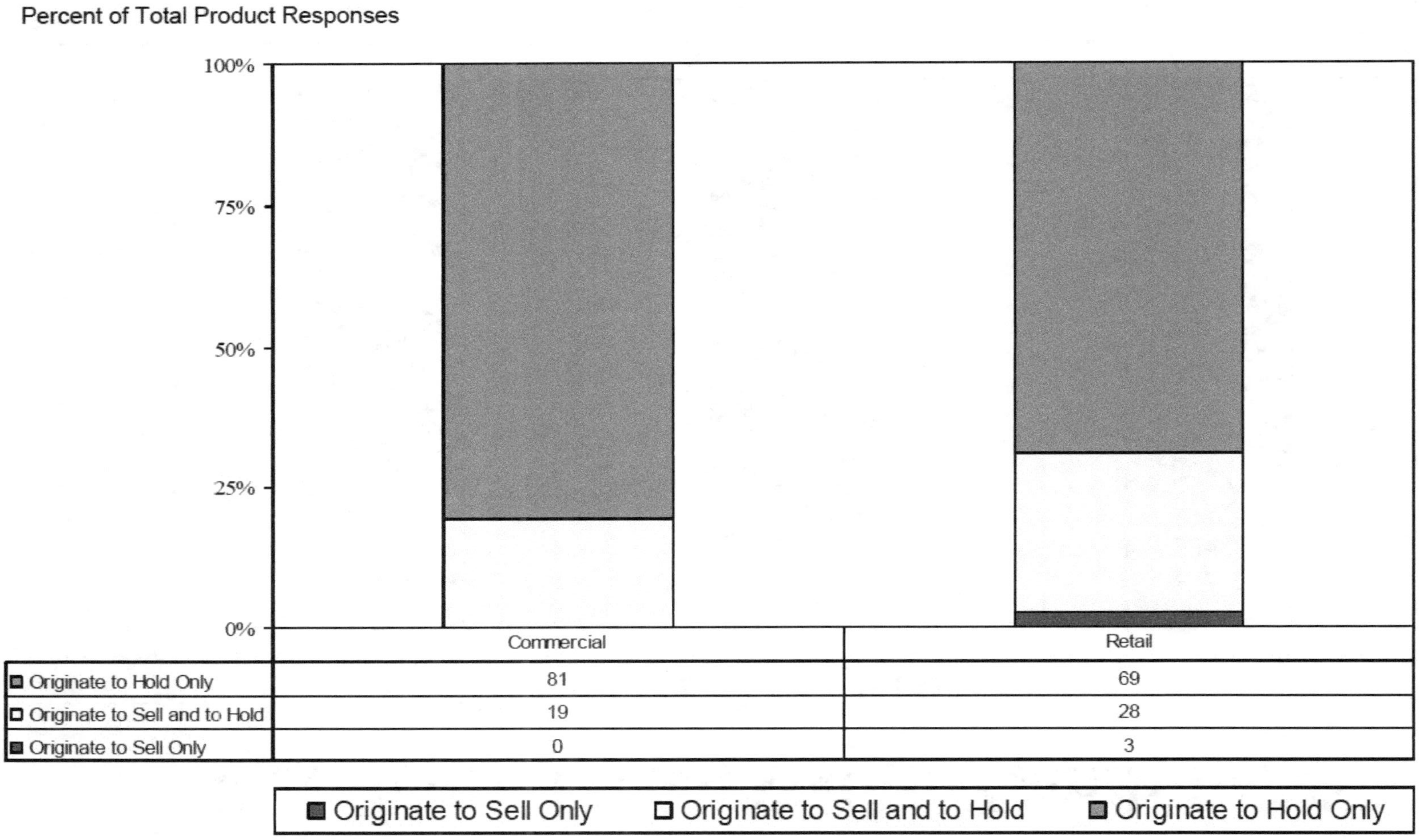

Percent of Total Product Responses

	Commercial	Retail
Originate to Hold Only	81	69
Originate to Sell and to Hold	19	28
Originate to Sell Only	0	3

■ Originate to Sell Only ☐ Originate to Sell and to Hold ■ Originate to Hold Only

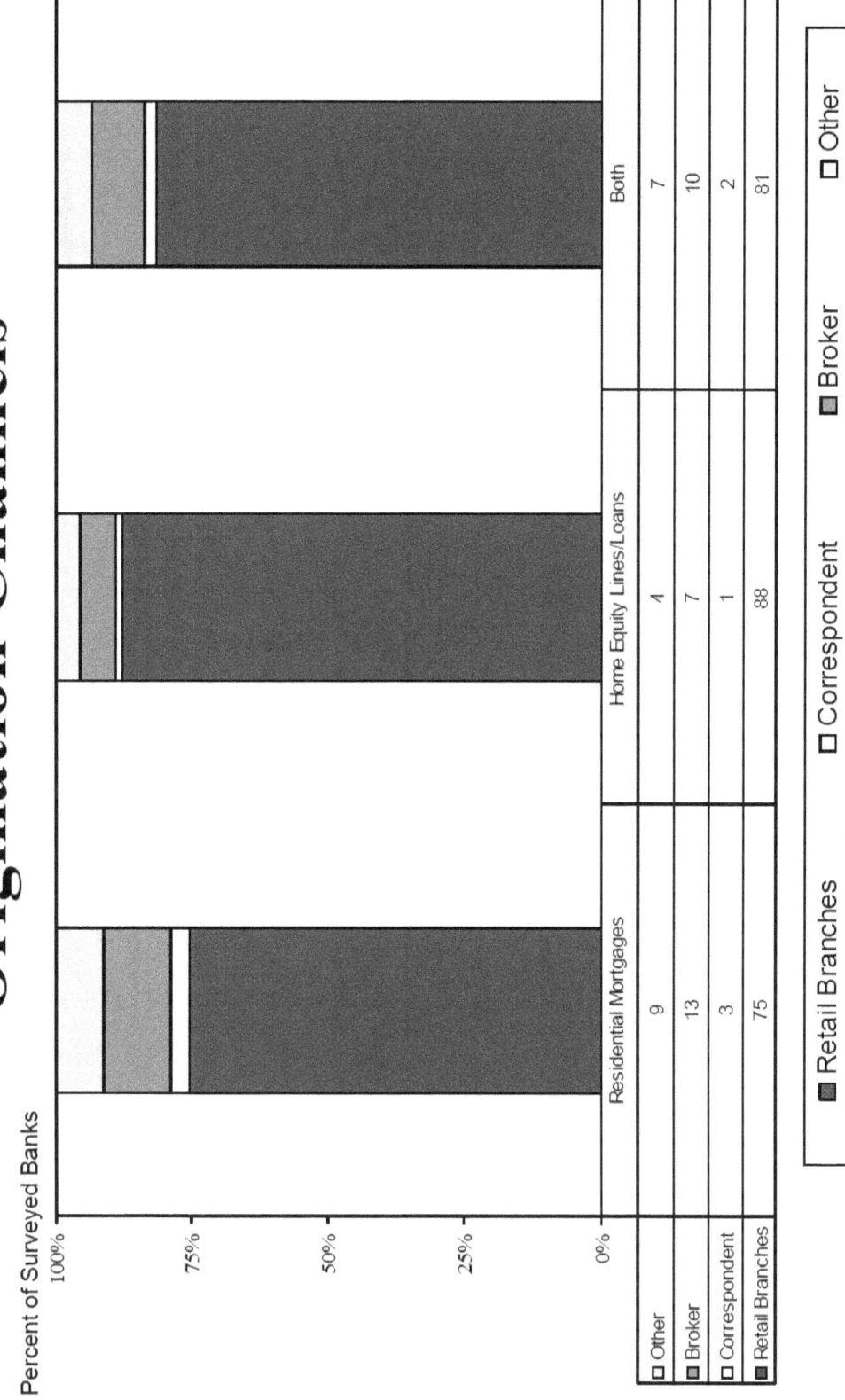

Residential Real Estate Lending Origination Channels

Percent of Surveyed Banks

	Residential Mortgages	Home Equity Lines/Loans	Both
Other	9	4	7
Broker	13	7	10
Correspondent	3	1	2
Retail Branches	75	88	81

■ Retail Branches ☐ Correspondent ■ Broker ☐ Other

Survey of Credit Underwriting 2008

Tables: Commercial Lending Portfolios

Agricultural Lending

Nineteen of the 62 banks in the survey were engaged in some form of agricultural lending.

Changes in Underwriting Standards in Agricultural Loan Portfolios
(Percent of Responses)

	Eased	Unchanged	Tightened
2000	3	71	26
2001	3	71	26
2002	0	70	30
2003	0	67	33
2004	0	93	7
2005	0	93	7
2006	5	95	0
2007	10	80	10
2008	0	95	5

Changes in the Level of Credit Risk in Agricultural Loan Portfolios
(Percent of Responses)

	Declined Significantly	Declined Somewhat	Unchanged	Increased Somewhat	Increased Significantly
2000	0	15	41	44	0
2001	0	17	43	34	6
2002	0	7	63	30	0
2003	0	11	48	41	0
2004	0	10	59	31	0
2005	4	17	69	10	0
2006	0	23	63	14	0
2007	0	0	55	45	0
2008	0	26	47	26	0
Future 12 Months	0	5	58	37	0

Asset-Based Loans

Twenty-three banks in the survey were engaged in asset-based lending.

Changes in Underwriting Standards in Asset-Based Loan Portfolios
(Percent of Responses)

	Eased	Unchanged	Tightened
2000	11	67	22
2001	5	53	42
2002	3	66	31
2003	0	58	42
2004	16	71	13
2005	30	67	3
2006	30	57	13
2007	25	68	7
2008	9	70	22

Changes in the Level of Credit Risk in Asset-Based Loan Portfolios
(Percent of Responses)

	Declined Significantly	Declined Somewhat	Unchanged	Increased Somewhat	Increased Significantly
2000	0	8	62	30	0
2001	5	8	42	45	0
2002	0	0	50	50	0
2003	3	26	42	29	0
2004	3	29	55	13	0
2005	0	24	52	24	0
2006	0	17	61	22	0
2007	0	14	43	43	0
2008	0	0	30	70	0
Future 12 Months	0	0	26	74	0

Commercial Leasing

Commercial leasing was offered by 14 of the banks in the survey.

Changes in Underwriting Standards in Commercial Leasing Portfolios
(Percent of Responses)

	Eased	Unchanged	Tightened
2006	12	76	12
2007	26	69	5
2008	7	50	43

Changes in the Level of Credit Risk in Commercial Leasing Portfolios
(Percent of Responses)

	Declined Significantly	Declined Somewhat	Unchanged	Increased Somewhat	Increased Significantly
2006	6	35	53	6	0
2007	0	16	63	21	0
2008	0	0	71	29	0
Future 12 Months	0	0	50	50	0

Commercial Real Estate Lending — Commercial Construction

Forty-nine of the banks in the survey were engaged in commercial construction lending.

Changes in Underwriting Standards in Commercial Construction Loan Portfolios
(Percent of Responses)

	Eased	Unchanged	Tightened
2003	2	61	37
2004	10	75	15
2005	29	63	8
2006	32	56	12
2007	28	59	13
2008	8	43	49

Changes in the Level of Credit Risk in Commercial Construction Loan Portfolios
(Percent of Responses)

	Declined Significantly	Declined Somewhat	Unchanged	Increased Somewhat	Increased Significantly
2003	0	7	46	42	5
2004	0	7	59	34	0
2005	2	5	65	28	0
2006	0	5	65	30	0
2007	0	2	48	49	1
2008	0	0	22	69	8
Future 12 Months	0	0	12	82	6

Commercial Real Estate Lending — Residential Construction

Forty-two of the banks in the survey were engaged in residential construction lending.

Changes in Underwriting Standards in Residential Construction Loan Portfolios
(Percent of Responses)

	Eased	Unchanged	Tightened
2003	0	76	24
2004	5	86	9
2005	21	72	7
2006	25	64	11
2007	17	50	33
2008	2	36	62

Changes in the Level of Credit Risk in Residential Construction Loan Portfolios
(Percent of Responses)

	Declined Significantly	Declined Somewhat	Unchanged	Increased Somewhat	Increased Significantly
2003	0	2	62	34	2
2004	0	4	76	18	2
2005	2	6	65	27	0
2006	0	2	52	46	0
2007	0	4	27	63	6
2008	0	0	7	48	45
Future 12 Months	0	2	12	62	24

Commercial Real Estate Lending — Other

Fifty-nine of the banks in the survey were engaged in other commercial real estate lending.

Changes in Underwriting Standards in Other Commercial Real Estate Loan Portfolios
(Percent of Responses)

	Eased	Unchanged	Tightened
2003	5	71	24
2004	8	83	9
2005	24	65	11
2006	32	60	8
2007	20	73	7
2008	2	73	25

Changes in the Level of Credit Risk in Other Commercial Real Estate Loan Portfolios
(Percent of Responses)

	Declined Significantly	Declined Somewhat	Unchanged	Increased Somewhat	Increased Significantly
2003	0	5	48	43	4
2004	0	12	66	20	2
2005	2	9	65	24	0
2006	1	10	55	34	0
2007	0	2	59	38	1
2008	0	2	39	58	2
Future 12 Months	0	0	17	81	2

International Lending

Only 10 of the banks in the survey were active in international lending.

Changes in Underwriting Standards in International Loan Portfolios
(Percent of Responses)

	Eased	Unchanged	Tightened
2000	14	72	14
2001	29	57	14
2002	11	61	28
2003	6	55	39
2004	11	61	28
2005	27	73	0
2006	30	70	0
2007	30	70	0
2008	10	60	30

Changes in the Level of Credit Risk in International Loan Portfolios
(Percent of Responses)

	Declined Significantly	Declined Somewhat	Unchanged	Increased Somewhat	Increased Significantly
2000	0	33	53	14	0
2001	0	14	53	33	0
2002	0	22	39	28	11
2003	0	6	55	33	6
2004	6	33	55	6	0
2005	0	20	73	7	0
2006	0	0	80	20	0
2007	0	0	70	30	0
2008	0	0	40	40	20
Future 12 Months	0	10	10	60	20

Middle Market Lending

Forty-eight of the banks in the survey were engaged in middle market lending.

Changes in Underwriting Standards in Middle Market Loan Portfolios
(Percent of Responses)

	Eased	Unchanged	Tightened
2000	18	66	16
2001	11	48	41
2002	0	60	40
2003	6	63	31
2004	14	81	5
2005	28	67	5
2006	31	66	3
2007	33	60	7
2008	6	69	25

Changes in the Level of Credit Risk in Middle Market Loan Portfolios
(Percent of Responses)

	Declined Significantly	Declined Somewhat	Unchanged	Increased Somewhat	Increased Significantly
2000	0	2	50	46	2
2001	0	2	35	59	4
2002	2	8	22	66	2
2003	0	13	39	44	4
2004	0	28	52	18	2
2005	4	26	54	16	0
2006	0	24	54	20	2
2007	0	5	51	44	0
2008	0	0	50	48	2
Future 12 Months	0	0	15	85	0

Small Business Lending

Thirty-six of the banks in the survey were lending in the small business market.

Changes in Underwriting Standards in Small Business Loan Portfolios
(Percent of Responses)

	Eased	Unchanged	Tightened
2000	8	73	19
2001	5	63	32
2002	2	66	32
2003	4	65	31
2004	11	74	15
2005	13	81	6
2006	19	76	5
2007	11	76	13
2008	11	72	17

Changes in the Level of Credit Risk in Small Business Loan Portfolios
(Percent of Responses)

	Declined Significantly	Declined Somewhat	Unchanged	Increased Somewhat	Increased Significantly
2000	0	3	72	22	3
2001	0	3	60	37	0
2002	0	2	56	40	2
2003	0	4	56	38	2
2004	0	15	72	13	0
2005	0	11	70	19	0
2006	0	5	71	22	2
2007	2	4	66	26	2
2008	0	3	36	58	3
Future 12 Months	3	0	22	72	3

Leveraged Loans

Fifteen of the banks in the survey provided leveraged loans.

Changes in Underwriting Standards in Leveraged Loan Portfolios
(Percent of Responses)

	Eased	Unchanged	Tightened
2000	35	45	20
2001	0	4	96
2002	0	44	56
2003	0	48	52
2004	15	85	0
2005	32	68	0
2006	61	31	8
2007	67	33	0
2008	20	20	60

Changes in the Level of Credit Risk in Leveraged Loan Portfolios
(Percent of Responses)

	Declined Significantly	Declined Somewhat	Unchanged	Increased Somewhat	Increased Significantly
2000	0	0	20	80	0
2001	0	4	8	46	42
2002	0	7	26	52	15
2003	10	33	28	29	0
2004	15	40	40	5	0
2005	5	27	58	5	5
2006	0	8	15	69	8
2007	0	13	34	53	0
2008	0	0	27	53	20
Future 12 Months	0	0	7	87	7

Large Corporate Loans

Thirty-four of the banks in the survey were active in the large corporate loan market.

Changes in Underwriting Standards in Large Corporate Loan Portfolios
(Percent of Responses)

	Eased	Unchanged	Tightened
2000	22	61	17
2001	0	34	66
2002	0	45	55
2003	3	49	48
2004	17	66	17
2005	32	68	0
2006	49	51	0
2007	40	60	0
2008	6	62	32

Changes in the Level of Credit Risk in Large Corporate Loan Portfolios
(Percent of Responses)

	Declined Significantly	Declined Somewhat	Unchanged	Increased Somewhat	Increased Significantly
2000	0	0	36	61	3
2001	0	6	17	63	14
2002	0	8	29	53	10
2003	5	27	33	30	5
2004	17	36	36	11	0
2005	5	27	49	19	0
2006	0	19	46	32	3
2007	0	8	57	35	0
2008	0	0	47	47	6
Future 12 Months	0	0	18	79	3

Hedge Funds (Direct Credit Exposure)

Only six of the banks in the survey were active in direct lending to hedge funds.

Changes in Underwriting Standards in Hedge Funds (Direct Credit Exposure)
(Percent of Responses)

	Eased	Unchanged	Tightened
2007	17	66	17
2008	0	100	0

Changes in the Level of Credit Risk in Hedge Funds (Direct Credit Exposure)
(Percent of Responses)

	Declined Significantly	Declined Somewhat	Unchanged	Increased Somewhat	Increased Significantly
2007	0	0	83	17	0
2008	0	0	83	17	0
Future 12 Months	0	0	67	17	17

Hedge Funds (Counterparty Credit Exposure)

Only seven of the banks in the survey had sizable counterparty credit exposures to hedge funds.

Changes in Underwriting Standards in Hedge Funds (Counterparty Credit Exposure)
(Percent of Responses)

	Eased	Unchanged	Tightened
2007	29	71	0
2008	0	29	71

Changes in the Level of Credit Risk in Hedge Funds (Counterparty Credit Exposure)
(Percent of Responses)

	Declined Significantly	Declined Somewhat	Unchanged	Increased Somewhat	Increased Significantly
2007	0	14	72	14	0
2008	0	14	29	43	14
Future 12 Months	0	29	29	29	14

Tables: Retail Lending Portfolios

Affordable Housing Lending

Thirty-one of the banks in the survey were reported to have made affordable housing loans.

Changes in Underwriting Standards in Affordable Housing Loan Portfolios
(Percent of Responses)

	Eased	Unchanged	Tightened
2000	10	84	6
2001	6	88	6
2002	3	91	6
2003	3	88	9
2004	6	86	8
2005	15	76	9
2006	3	97	0
2007	6	88	6
2008	3	74	23

Changes in the Level of Credit Risk in Affordable Housing Loan Portfolios
(Percent of Responses)

	Declined Significantly	Declined Somewhat	Unchanged	Increased Somewhat	Increased Significantly
2000	0	6	83	11	0
2001	2	2	88	8	0
2002	0	6	73	21	0
2003	0	9	76	15	0
2004	0	9	82	9	0
2005	0	6	79	15	0
2006	0	3	86	11	0
2007	0	0	88	12	0
2008	0	0	58	35	6
Future 12 Months	0	0	48	48	3

Credit Card Lending

Seventeen of the banks in the survey were engaged in credit card lending.

Changes in Underwriting Standards in Credit Card Loan Portfolios
(Percent of Responses)

	Eased	Unchanged	Tightened
2000	9	75	16
2001	16	60	24
2002	12	66	22
2003	19	62	19
2004	18	61	21
2005	7	74	19
2006	19	56	25
2007	16	79	5
2008	18	47	35

Changes in the Level of Credit Risk in Credit Card Loan Portfolios
(Percent of Responses)

	Declined Significantly	Declined Somewhat	Unchanged	Increased Somewhat	Increased Significantly
2000	0	16	66	16	2
2001	8	5	57	27	3
2002	0	6	54	31	9
2003	0	22	48	30	0
2004	0	11	61	25	3
2005	0	15	67	18	0
2006	0	0	56	44	0
2007	0	11	63	26	0
2008	0	0	35	65	0
Future 12 Months	0	0	29	71	0

Other Direct Consumer Lending

Thirty-two of the banks in the survey were engaged in other direct consumer lending.

Changes in Underwriting Standards in Other Direct Consumer Loan Portfolios
(Percent of Responses)

	Eased	Unchanged	Tightened
2000	10	78	12
2001	7	73	20
2002	2	67	31
2003	8	68	24
2004	3	86	11
2005	6	82	12
2006	3	91	6
2007	8	87	5
2008	6	72	22

Changes in the Level of Credit Risk in Other Direct Consumer Loan Portfolios
(Percent of Responses)

	Declined Significantly	Declined Somewhat	Unchanged	Increased Somewhat	Increased Significantly
2000	0	9	74	15	2
2001	0	7	71	20	2
2002	2	6	67	25	0
2003	2	17	72	7	2
2004	2	13	78	7	0
2005	0	8	82	10	0
2006	0	3	88	9	0
2007	0	3	87	10	0
2008	0	3	59	38	0
Future 12 Months	0	0	50	50	0

Home Equity — Conventional Lending

Fifty-two of the banks in the survey offered the conventional home equity lending product.

Changes in Underwriting Standards in Home Equity — Conventional Loan Portfolios
(Percent of Responses)

	Eased	Unchanged	Tightened
2000	23	64	13
2001	7	70	23
2002	0	74	26
2003	18	63	19
2004	13	77	10
2005	27	62	11
2006	34	64	2
2007	19	65	16
2008	2	46	52

Changes in the Level of Credit Risk in Home Equity — Conventional Loan Portfolios
(Percent of Responses)

	Declined Significantly	Declined Somewhat	Unchanged	Increased Somewhat	Increased Significantly
2000	0	5	73	20	2
2001	0	11	74	13	2
2002	0	7	71	22	0
2003	4	4	69	23	0
2004	0	6	79	13	2
2005	0	7	78	15	0
2006	0	0	69	29	2
2007	0	0	63	34	3
2008	0	0	29	52	19
Future 12 Months	0	0	23	71	6

Home Equity — High-LTV Lending

Eighteen of the banks in the survey offered the high LTV home equity lending product.

Changes in Underwriting Standards in Home Equity — High-LTV Loan Portfolios
(Percent of Responses)

	Eased	Unchanged	Tightened
2000	21	55	24
2001	11	54	35
2002	0	56	44
2003	7	68	25
2004	18	71	11
2005	24	56	20
2006	37	63	0
2007	22	61	17
2008	6	6	89

Changes in the Level of Credit Risk in Home Equity — High-LTV Loan Portfolios
(Percent of Responses)

	Declined Significantly	Declined Somewhat	Unchanged	Increased Somewhat	Increased Significantly
2000	0	13	58	24	5
2001	5	11	62	16	6
2002	0	12	40	44	4
2003	0	11	50	36	3
2004	0	18	61	18	3
2005	0	4	72	24	0
2006	0	0	63	37	0
2007	0	6	39	55	0
2008	0	0	0	56	44
Future 12 Months	0	0	17	67	17

Indirect Consumer Lending

Twenty-five of the banks in the survey were engaged in indirect consumer lending.

Changes in Underwriting Standards in Indirect Consumer Loan Portfolios
(Percent of Responses)

	Eased	Unchanged	Tightened
2000	7	60	33
2001	7	63	30
2002	0	72	28
2003	5	65	30
2004	11	60	29
2005	25	61	14
2006	35	52	13
2007	16	75	9
2008	20	56	24

Changes in the Level of Credit Risk in Indirect Consumer Loan Portfolios
(Percent of Responses)

	Declined Significantly	Declined Somewhat	Unchanged	Increased Somewhat	Increased Significantly
2000	7	16	55	22	0
2001	2	21	39	33	5
2002	3	13	38	43	3
2003	5	20	47	28	0
2004	0	26	60	14	0
2005	3	19	67	8	3
2006	6	10	48	36	0
2007	0	3	87	10	0
2008	0	4	36	60	0
Future 12 Months	0	8	16	76	0

Residential Real Estate Lending

Fifty-five of the banks in the survey were engaged in residential real estate lending.

Changes in Underwriting Standards in Residential Real Estate Loan Portfolios
(Percent of Responses)

	Eased	Unchanged	Tightened
2000	7	85	8
2001	12	72	16
2002	4	83	13
2003	2	86	12
2004	7	86	7
2005	22	73	5
2006	26	69	5
2007	19	67	14
2008	0	44	56

Changes in the Level of Credit Risk in Residential Real Estate Loan Portfolios
(Percent of Responses)

	Declined Significantly	Declined Somewhat	Unchanged	Increased Somewhat	Increased Significantly
2000	0	3	83	12	2
2001	0	9	76	15	0
2002	0	8	68	24	0
2003	0	12	74	12	2
2004	0	6	92	2	0
2005	0	3	73	24	0
2006	0	7	69	24	0
2007	2	6	59	33	0
2008	2	0	38	55	5
Future 12 Months	0	4	33	62	2